Team Spirit

Becca Heddle

Illustrated by **Isabella Grott**

OXFORD
UNIVERSITY PRESS

Letter from the Author

I'm Becca, and I wrote this book. I'm no good at sports, but I do sing with friends – that's my favourite kind of team.

I've also written lots of books and guess what? Books take teamwork, too! Once I've written the words, editors check it all makes sense, and a designer creates the look of each page. Then photo researchers and artists work to get every picture right. And this is all before the printing team gets involved to turn our ideas into a real book.

I love working as part of a team, because we can do so much more as a team than I could do on my own.

What kinds of team do you like to be part of?

Becca Heddle

Contents

What is a Team? 4

Sports Teams 6

Life-saving Teams 10

Performing Teams 14

Virtual Teams 18

Which Team Member Are You?............ 20

Brilliant Teams! 22

Glossary 23

Index 24

The glossary

Some words in this book are in **bold**. When you read a **bold** word, think about what it means. If you don't know, you can look it up in the glossary at the end of the book.

What is a Team?

Have you ever played or worked in a team?

Whenever people work or play together, they make up a team – but the word 'team' can mean lots of different things. It's not just about sports teams!

How many different types of team can you think of?

This team is building a house. It's a complicated job, so each team member needs different skills.

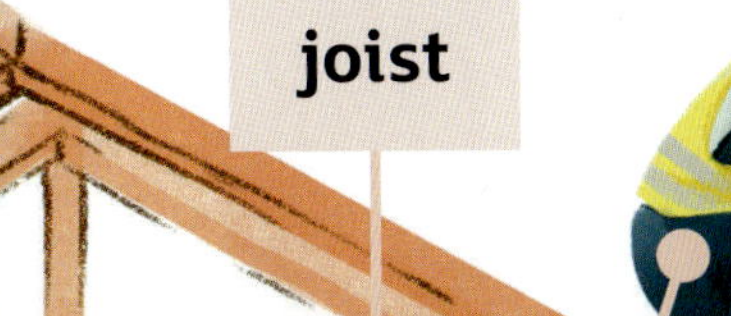

carpenter: makes things out of wood, like floorboards and joists

site manager: makes sure the project is completed safely and on time

plumber: puts in pipes to bring water to the house

bricklayer: builds walls with bricks and mortar

electrician: fits electrical equipment such as cables, plugs and sockets

Sports Teams

Gymnasts and divers train in teams, but they usually compete on their own. Only one person can win most events. However, team members still support each other!

Are there any other sports where people train in a team but compete on their own?

Sometimes it depends! Aryna Sabalenka and Elise Mertens work together as a team to win doubles tennis matches. They also compete *against* each other in singles tennis matches!

Can you think of a time where you have worked with a friend, and a time when you have competed against them?

A football team is different. The team members have different roles to play, but none of them can win on their own. When they win, the whole team wins. When they lose, they help each other to be **resilient** and keep training for the next match.

A football team on the pitch ...

Attackers move the ball up the pitch and score goals.

Midfielders are good at attacking and defending. They hold the team together.

Defenders help their team to get the ball and keep it away from their goal.

The goalkeeper needs quick reactions to stop the ball going in their net!

... and off the pitch

The team's manager decides on the team's **tactics** and chooses who will play.

Substitute players wait by the pitch. They have to be ready to play and able to cope with disappointment if they don't.

A **physiotherapist** assesses injuries and helps players to recover from them.

The kit manager looks after the team's clothes, boots and equipment.

Life-saving Teams

Firefighters

A firefighting team has to work under pressure. Firefighters have to rush to **emergencies** and accidents, and solve problems quickly. Training and planning are vital.

When they arrive, the **crew** first works out how to tackle the situation. Then everyone follows their leader's orders, to **coordinate** their efforts and save lives.

OK everyone, what we're going to do is ...

Why do you think all firefighters have to be physically fit?

Training together helps firefighters to trust each other.

After an emergency, the team members talk together about what happened, what each of them did and how they feel about it. This helps them to cope with working in dangerous and upsetting situations.

The story of a paramedic call-out

The work of an ambulance crew depends on skills, speed and excellent communication. This is how everyone works together to help someone.

A cyclist has been injured in a road accident. Someone who saw what happened calls the emergency services.

1

2

The call handler keeps the caller calm. If an ambulance is needed, they pass on information to the **paramedics**.

The emergency care assistant drives the ambulance quickly and safely. They then help the paramedics with getting more information and giving emergency first aid.

3

4

The paramedics use equipment or medicine to help keep the patient safe until they reach hospital.

At the hospital, the paramedics explain everything that has happened so the doctors can treat the patient quickly.

5

Performing Teams

A concert team

Have you ever seen a music concert – either live or on television? Normally you see only the band, but other teams make sure everything goes smoothly.

The lighting crew sets up all the lights and controls them.

The backline crew keep the performers' instruments and equipment in perfect condition.

The sound engineer mixes the sound from all the microphones and instruments, so the audience hears everything properly.

The tour manager handles the travel arrangements and makes sure everyone gets paid.

What could happen if they didn't do their jobs well?

the lighting crew

the backline crew

the sound engineer

the tour manager

Putting on a show

Putting on a play needs another combination of teams, all working at the same time.

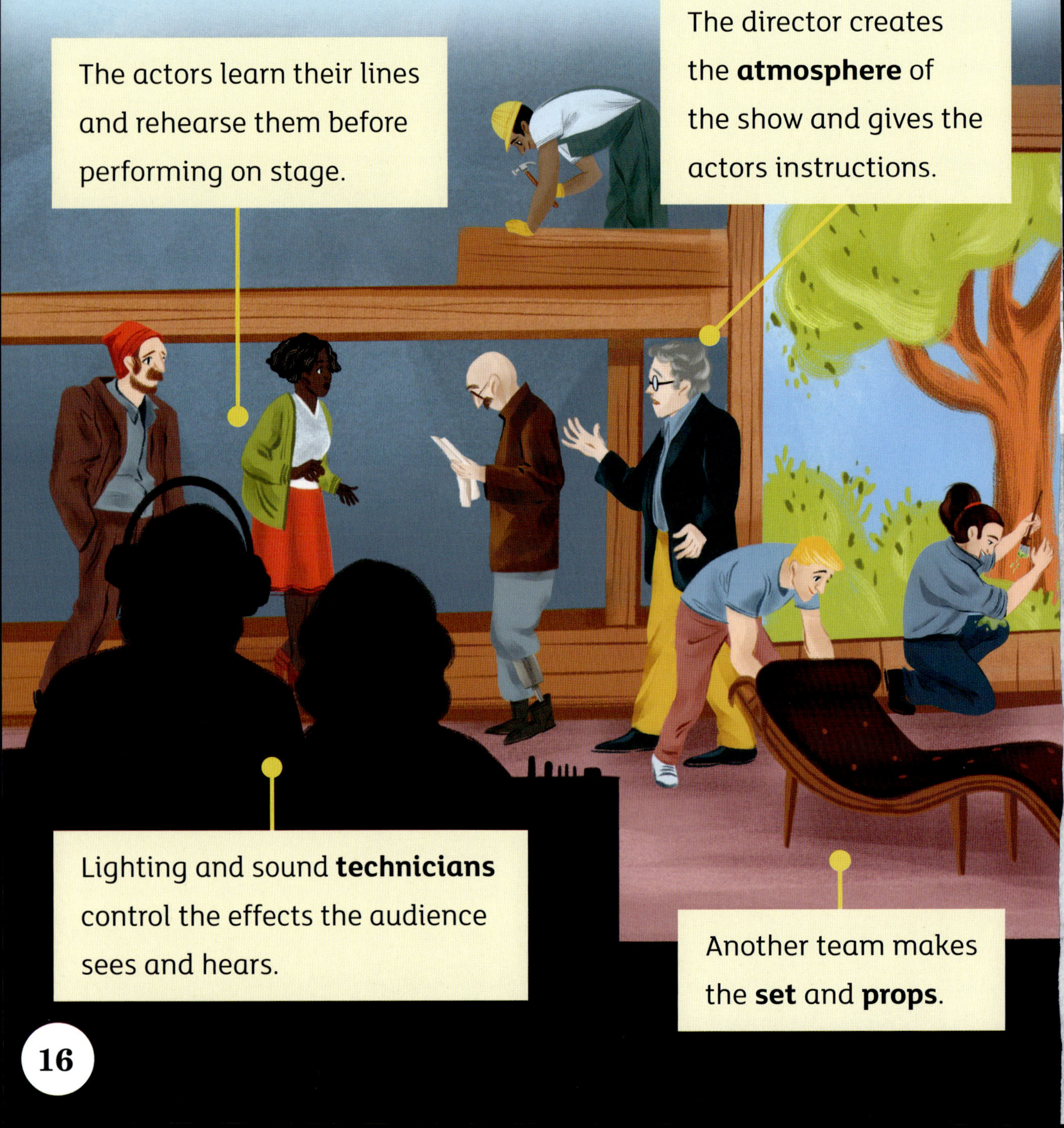

The actors learn their lines and rehearse them before performing on stage.

The director creates the **atmosphere** of the show and gives the actors instructions.

Lighting and sound **technicians** control the effects the audience sees and hears.

Another team makes the **set** and **props**.

The wardrobe team designs and then makes or buys costumes for the characters.

Hair and make-up artists make sure the actors look right.

The stage manager makes sure all the teams work together, so everything happens at the right time.

The front-of-house team sells tickets and helps audience members.

It's showtime!

Virtual Teams

Some teams work towards the same goal, but never meet! Lots of people do the same thing and mainly coordinate their efforts online.

Knits for Nature is a worldwide team of knitters. They started by making jumpers for penguins affected by oil spills.

Volunteers for the Snuggles Project make blankets to comfort animals in rescue shelters. The charity keeps a list of rescue shelters around the world. The blanket-makers send their blankets to their closest shelter.

For over twenty years, volunteers for SETI@home ran programs on their computers, to help look for evidence of life on other planets. SETI stands for 'search for **extra-terrestrial** intelligence'.

Which Team Member Are You?

Your school are organizing a cake sale to raise money for charity. How do you fit into the team?

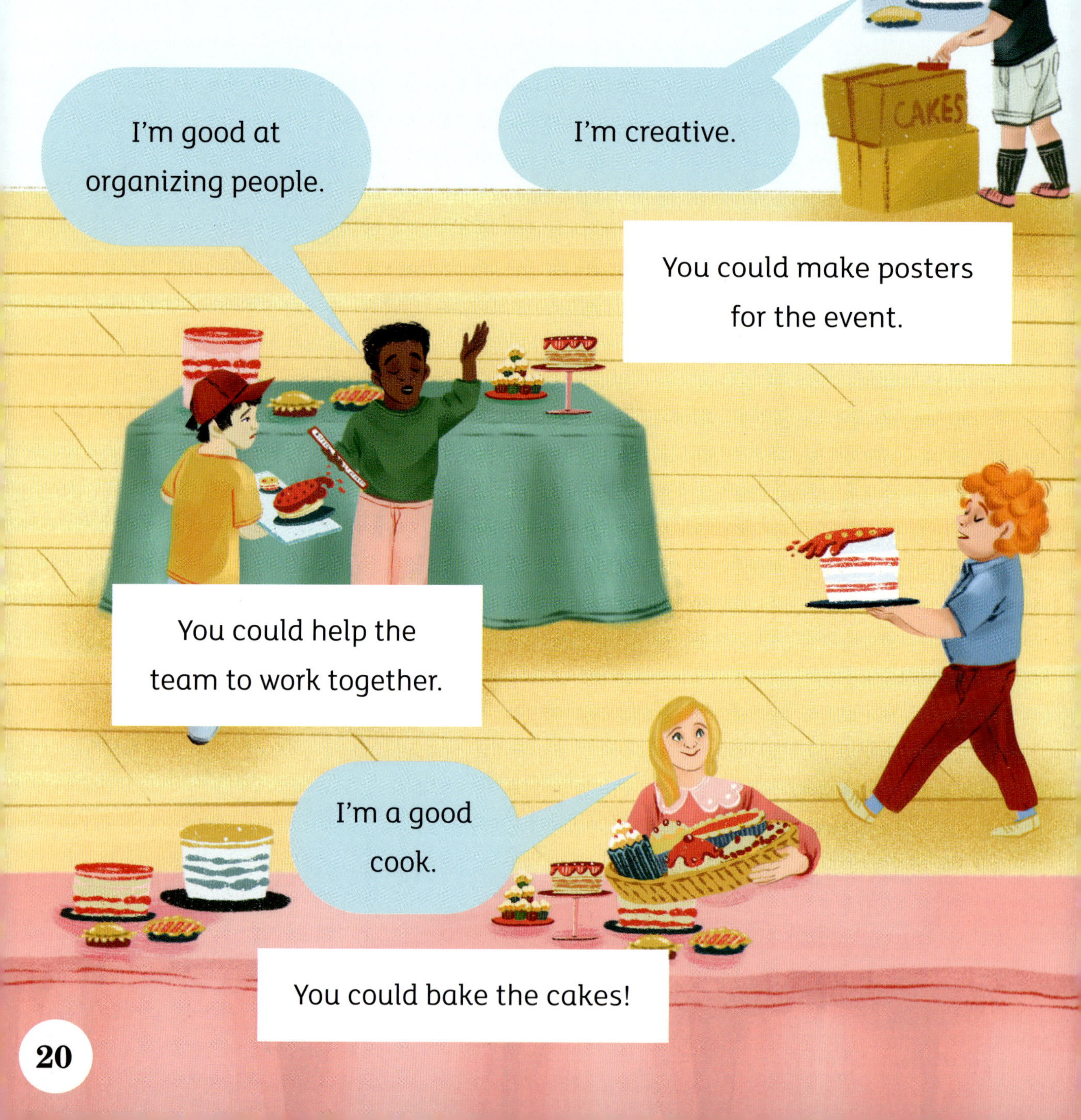

I'm good at organizing people.

You could help the team to work together.

I'm creative.

You could make posters for the event.

I'm a good cook.

You could bake the cakes!

I'm quick
at maths.
I don't mind following
instructions.
You'll be a really
useful helper.
You could collect and
count the money.
I just like
eating cake.
I've got loads
of energy.
Come and
buy some!
You could help tidy
up afterwards.

Brilliant Teams!

Every member of a team is important.

Ideally, team members all work together and take care of each other when things go wrong. When everything goes well, teams celebrate together.

What qualities do people need to work in a team? How can you practise teamwork this week?

Glossary

atmosphere: the feeling or mood

coordinate: to make different things work together

crew: a group of people who work closely together

emergencies: serious, unexpected situations in which help is needed

extra-terrestrial: not from Earth or its atmosphere

joist: a long piece of wood, concrete or metal used horizontally to support a floor or ceiling

mortar: a mixture of sand, cement and water, used to stick bricks together

paramedics: people trained to give emergency medical care, usually outside a hospital

physiotherapist: someone trained to treat people using massage and exercises

props: items used by performers taking part in a play, show or film

resilient: to be able to recover quickly from setbacks

set: walls, furniture and background for a play, show or film

substitute: a replacement

tactics: actions that form part of a plan

technicians: people with technical skills in subjects like science or engineering

Index

build 5
communication 12
help 7–9, 11–13, 17–23
manager 5, 9, 15, 17
perform 14–17, 23
skills 5, 8–13, 15–21, 23
sports 4, 6–9
support 6, 11, 15, 21
team member 5–9, 11, 20–22
train 6–7, 10–11, 23
volunteer 19